Homestead Poetry

ISBN: 979-8-218-36687-2

On the Homestead
by Christine Zell

As the sun rises on the homestead
you'll hear the rooster crow.
A long day awaits us
as we perform the routine we know.

We feed the chickens, gather their eggs,
which we'll need so we're all fed.
We'll go inside, gather supplies
for our delicious homemade bread.

We'll tend to the garden;
we'll water it and weed.
The vegetables are plentiful
and perfect for the soup we need.

We'll can, we'll bake, we'll cook,
thankful for all we've been given.
As the sun sets on the homestead
that we're so blessed to live in.

Tall Nettles

by Edward Thomas

Tall nettles cover up, as they have done
These many springs, the rusty harrow, the plough
Long worn out, and the roller made of stone:
Only the elm butt tops the nettles now.

This corner of the farmyard I like most:
As well as any bloom upon a flower
I like the dust on the nettles, never lost
Except to prove the sweetness of a shower.

We Have a Little Garden
by Helen Beatrix Potter

We have a little garden,
A garden of our own,
And every day we water there
The seeds that we have sown.

We love our little garden,
And tend it with such care,
You will not find a faded leaf
Or blighted blossom there.

Chanticleer

by Katherine Tynan Hinkson

Of all the birds from East to West
That tuneful are and dear,
I love that farmyard bird the best,
They call him Chanticleer.

Gold plume and copper plume,
Comb of scarlet gay;
'Tis he that scatters night and gloom,
And whistles back the day!

He is the sun's brave herald
That, ringing his blithe horn,
Calls round a world dew-pearled
The heavenly airs of morn.

O clear gold, shrill and bold!
He calls through creeping mist
The mountains from the night and cold
To rose and amethyst.

He sets the birds to singing,
And calls the flowers to rise;
The morning cometh, bringing
Sweet sleep to heavy eyes.

Gold plume and silver plume,
Comb of coral gay;
'Tis he packs off the night and gloom,
And summons home the day!

Black fear he sends it flying,
Black care he drives afar;
And creeping shadows sighing
Before the morning star.

The birds of all the forest
Have dear and pleasant cheer,
But yet I hold the rarest
The farmyard Chanticleer.

Red cock or black cock,
Gold cock or white,
The flower of all the feathered flock,
He whistles back the light!

All the Pretty Little Horses
by Dorothy Scarborough

Hush you bye, don't you cry,
Go to sleepy, little baby.
when you wake,
You shall have,
all the pretty little horses.

Blacks and Bays,
dapples and grays,
Coach and six a little horses.
Hush-a-by, Don't you cry,
Go to sleep, my little baby.

Milking Time

by Elizabeth Madox Roberts

When supper time is almost come,
But not quite here, I cannot wait,
And so I take my china mug
And go down by the milking gate.

The cow is always eating shucks
And spilling off the little silk.
Her purple eyes are big and soft–
She always smells like milk.

And Father takes my mug from me,
And then he makes the stream come out.
I see it going in my mug
And foaming all about.

And when it's piling very high,
And when some little streams commence
To run and drip along the sides,
He hands it to me through the fence.

Grape Jam
Strawberry Jam

Canning Time
by Edgar Albert Guest

There's a wondrous smell of spices
In the kitchen,
Most bewitchin';
There are fruits cut into slices
That just set the palate itchin';
There's the sound of spoon on platter
And the rattle and the clatter;
And a bunch of kids are hastin'
To the splendid joy of tastin':
It's the fragrant time of year
When fruit-cannin' days are here.
There's a good wife gayly smilin'
And perspirin'
Some, and tirin';
And while jar on jar she's pilin'
And the necks o' them she's wirin'

I'm a-sittin' here an' dreamin'
Of the kettles that are steamin',
And the cares that have been troublin'
All have vanished in the bubblin'.
I am happy that I'm here
At the cannin' time of year.
Lord, I'm sorry for the feller
That is missin'
All the hissin'
Of the juices, red and yeller,
And can never sit and listen
To the rattle and the clatter
Of the sound of spoon on platter.
I am sorry for the single,
For they miss the thrill and tingle
Of the splendid time of year
When the cannin' days are here.

A Bird Came Down the Walk
by Emily Dickinson

A Bird, came down the Walk -
He did not know I saw -
He bit an Angle Worm in halves
And ate the fellow, raw,

And then, he drank a Dew
From a convenient Grass -
And then hopped sidewise to the Wall
To let a Beetle pass -

He glanced with rapid eyes,
That hurried all abroad -
They looked like frightened Beads, I thought,
He stirred his Velvet Head. -

Like one in danger, Cautious,
I offered him a Crumb,
And he unrolled his feathers,
And rowed him softer Home -

Than Oars divide the Ocean,
Too silver for a seam,
Or Butterflies, off Banks of Noon,
Leap, plashless as they swim.

Weaving
by Florence May Gibbs

My life is but a weaving
Between my God and me;
I may but choose the colors—
He worketh steadily.
Full oft he weaveth sorrow;
And I in foolish pride,
Forget he sees the upper,
And I the under side!

I choose my strands all golden,
And watch for woven stars;
I murmur when the pattern
Is set in blurs and mars.
I cannot yet remember
Whose hands the shuttles guide;
And that my stars are shining
Upon the upper side.

I choose my thread all crimson,
And wait for flowers to bloom,
For warp and woof to blossom
Upon that mighty loom.
Full oft I seek them vainly,
And fret for them denied—
Though flowering wreaths and garlands,
May deck the upper side.

My life is but a weaving
Between my God and me;
I see the seams, the tangles—
The fair design sees He.
Then let me wait in patience
And blindness; satisfied
To make the pattern lovely
Upon the upper side.

About the Author

Christine Zell is a mother of four and a wife to her high school sweetheart. She owns a homeschool curriculum company, Rabbit Trails Homeschool. Christine loves picture books and using literature based curriculum in her homeschool. She lives in Ohio on a small homestead with her husband, four children, two dogs, twelve chickens, and a leopard gecko.

About the Illustrator

Ethan Zell is 15 years old and is a homeschool student. This is the second book Ethan has illustrated. He enjoys running on his cross country and track teams. He hopes to become an entreprenuer.

www.ingramcontent.com/pod-product-compliance
Lightning Source LLC
Chambersburg PA
CBHW041827110726
48006CB00019B/2543